SLOTHS

COLORING BOOK

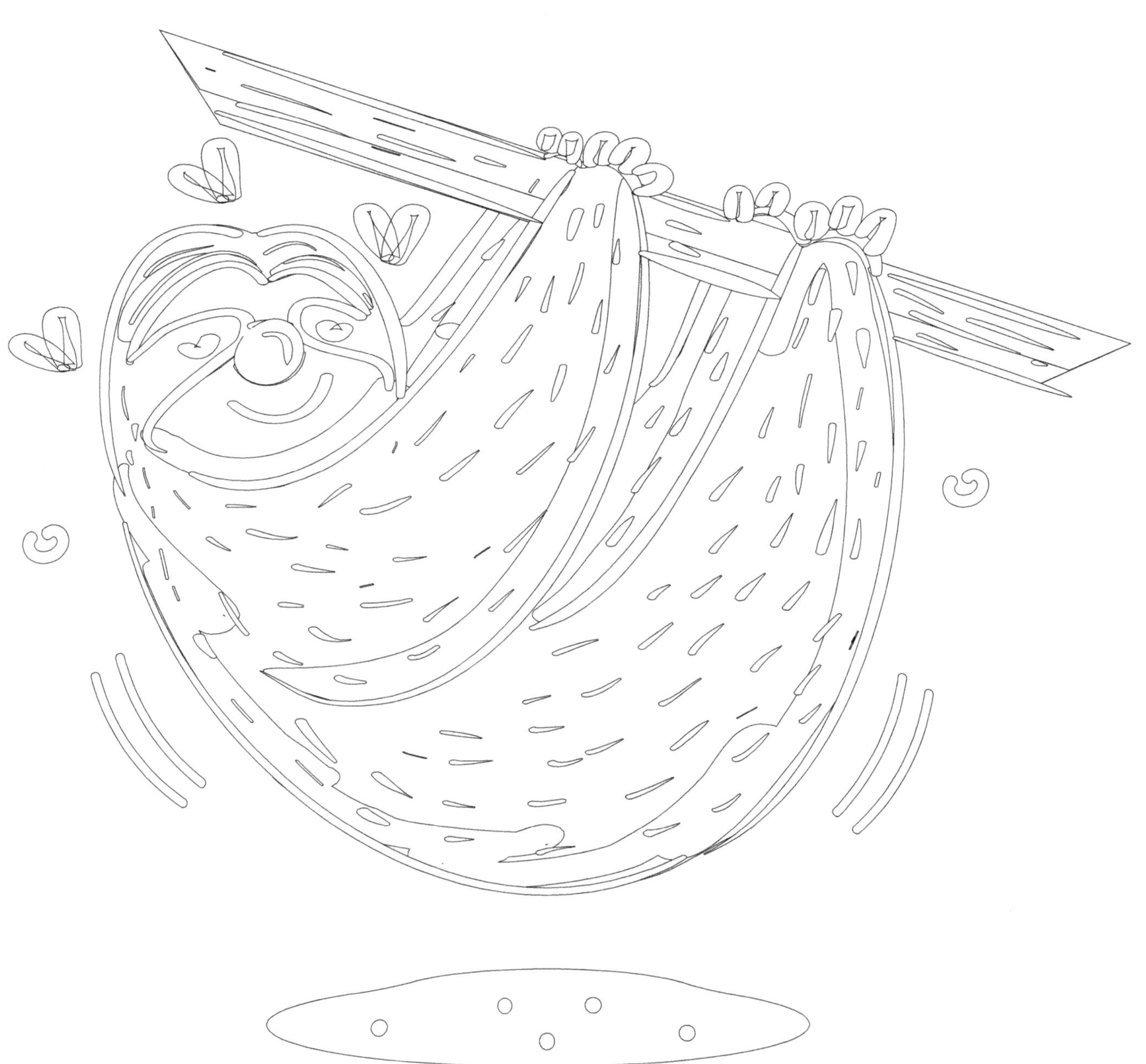

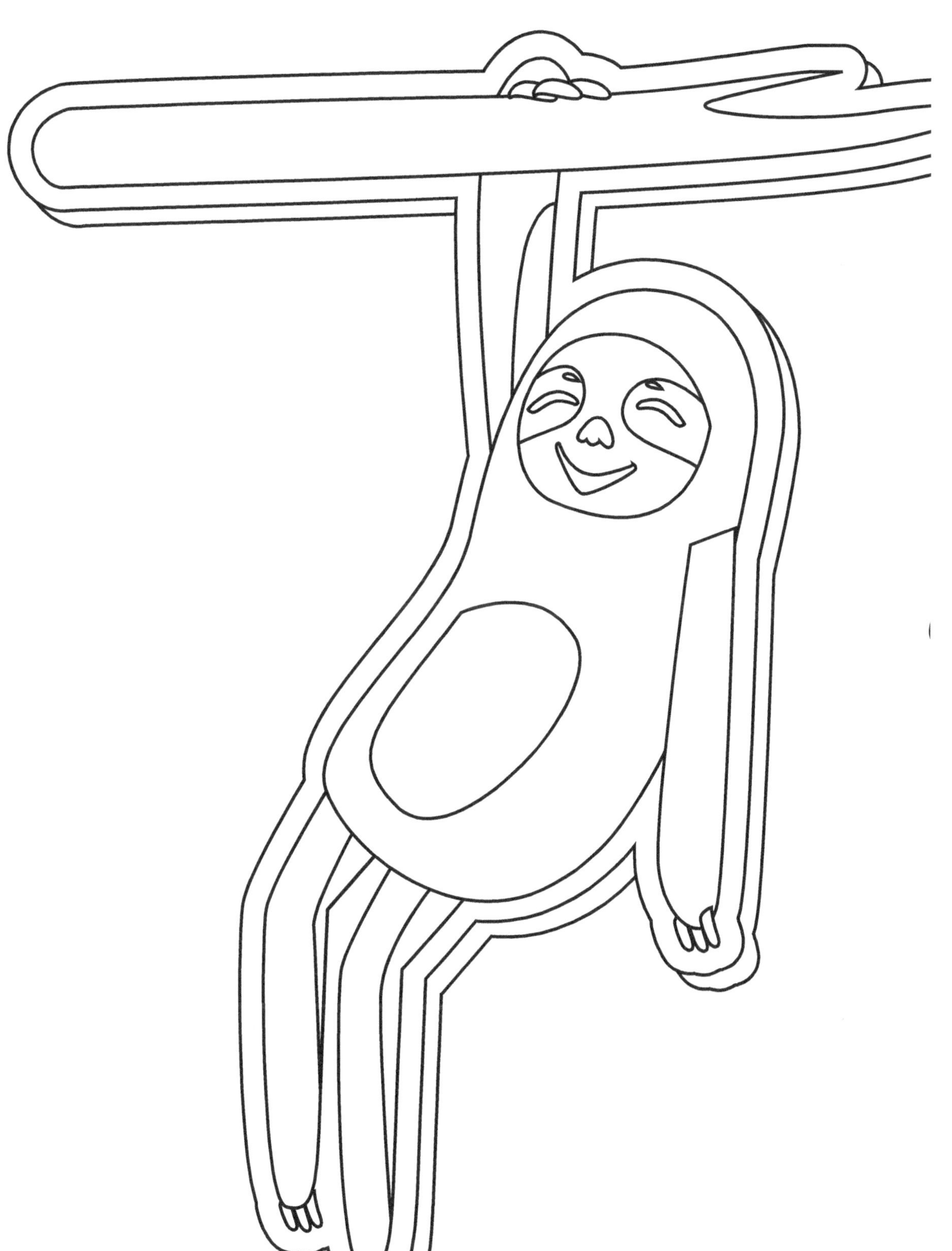

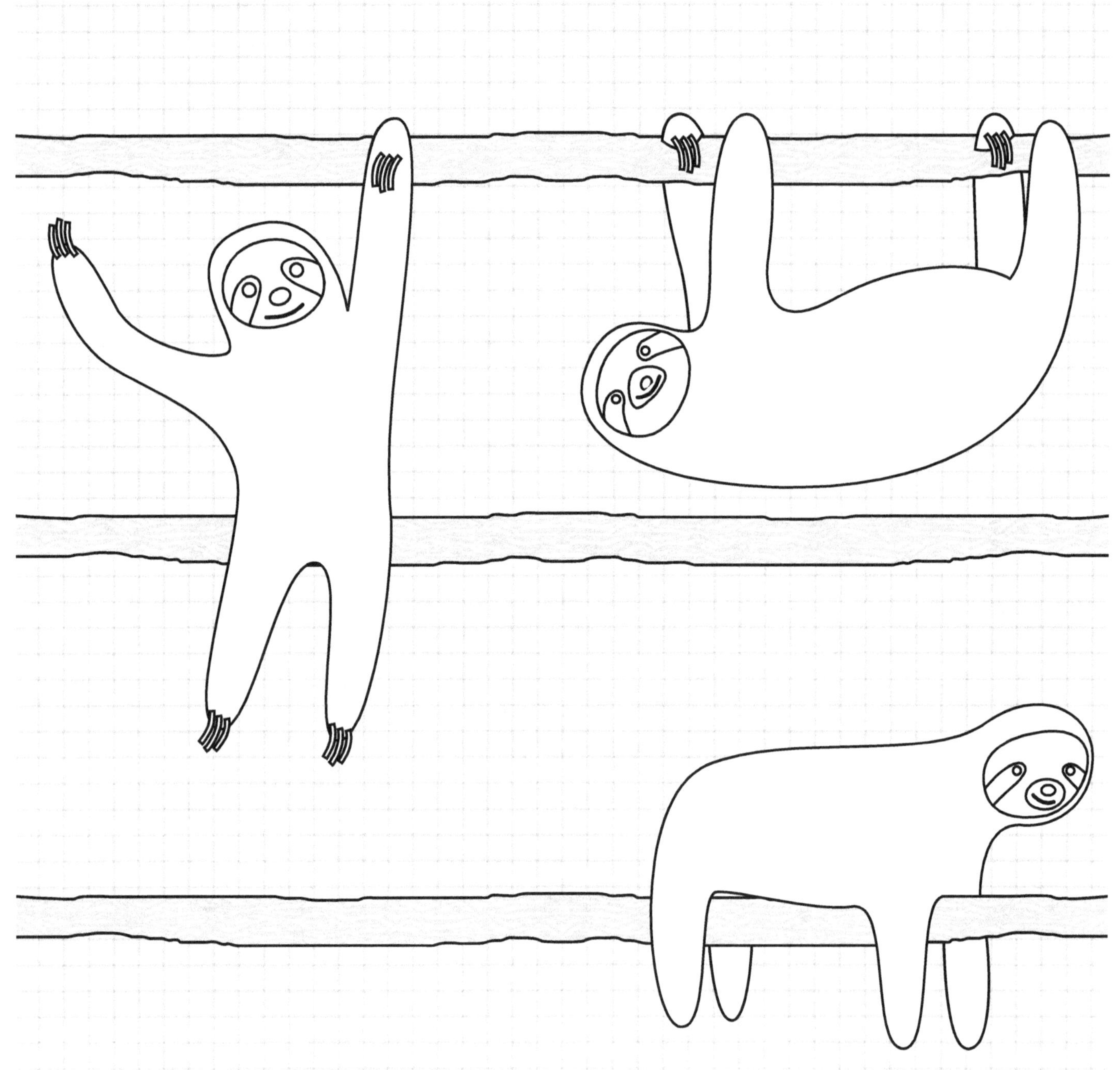

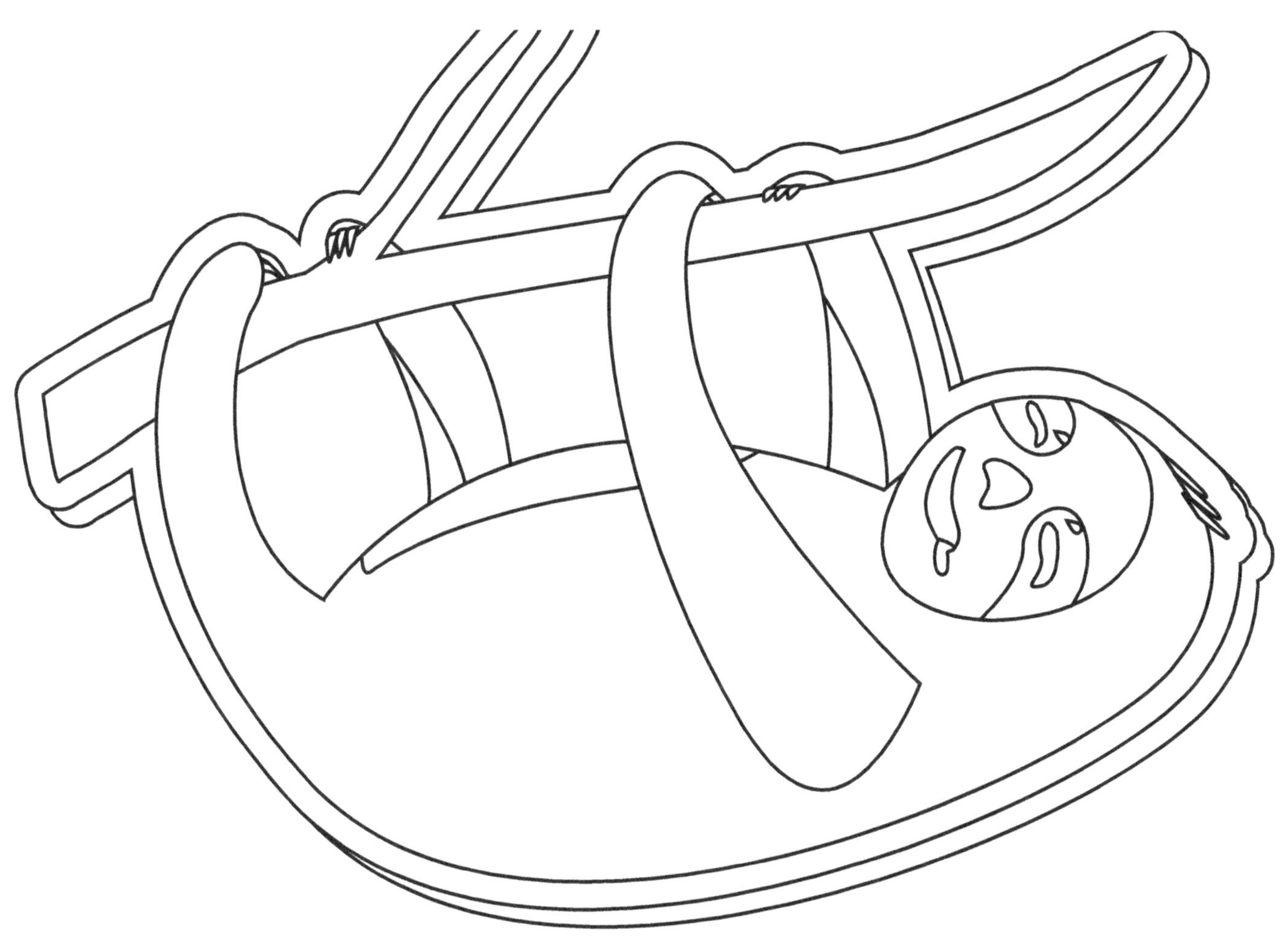

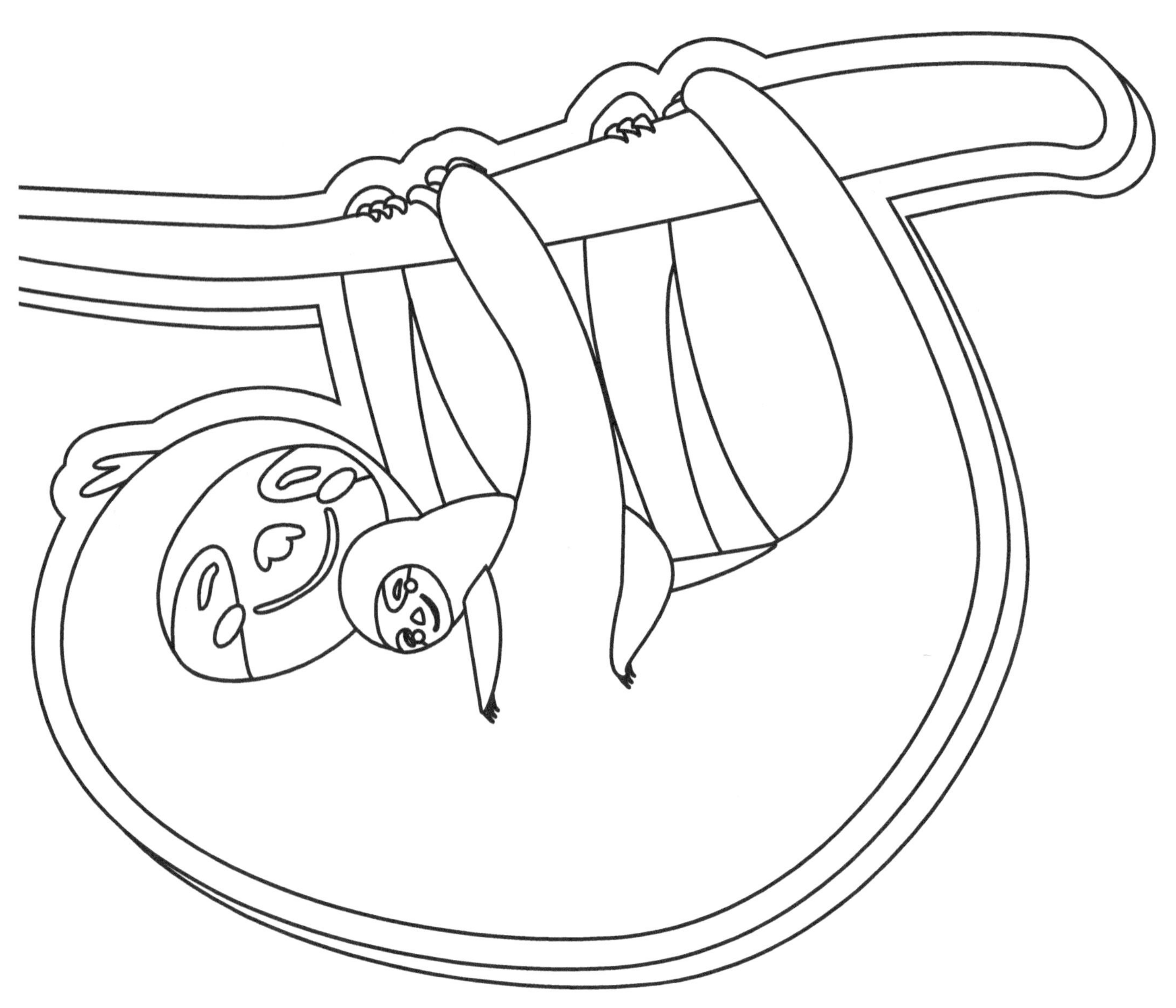

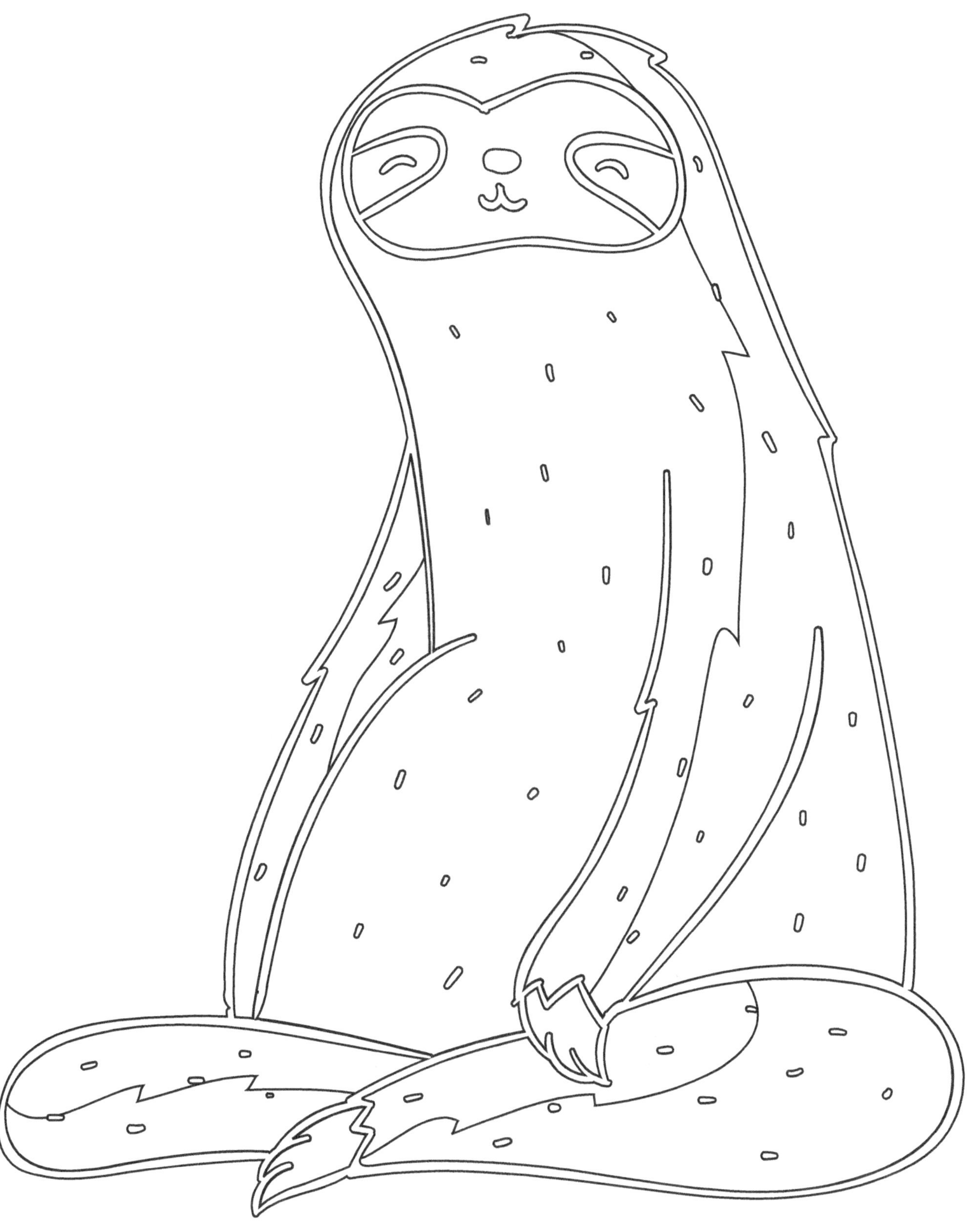

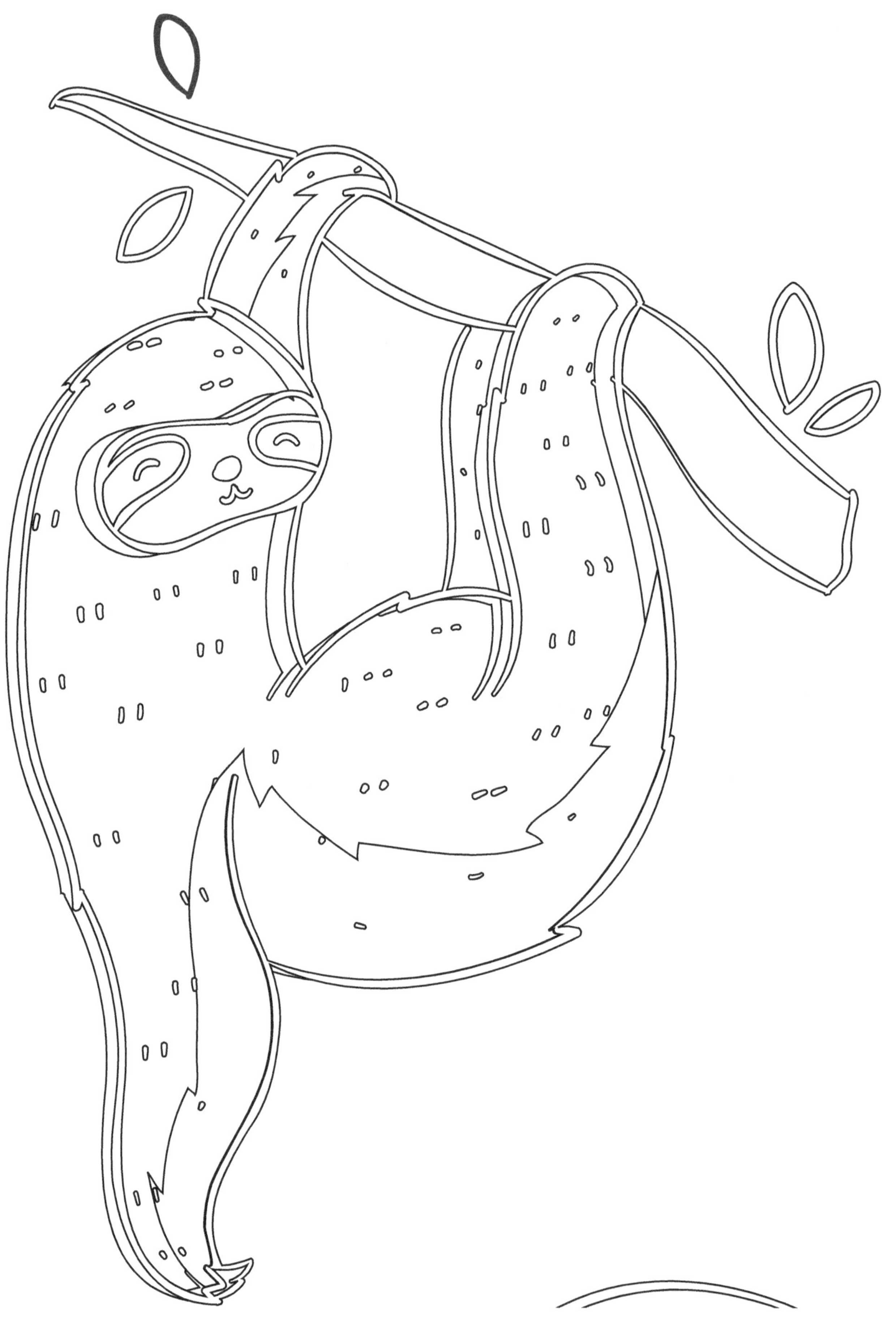

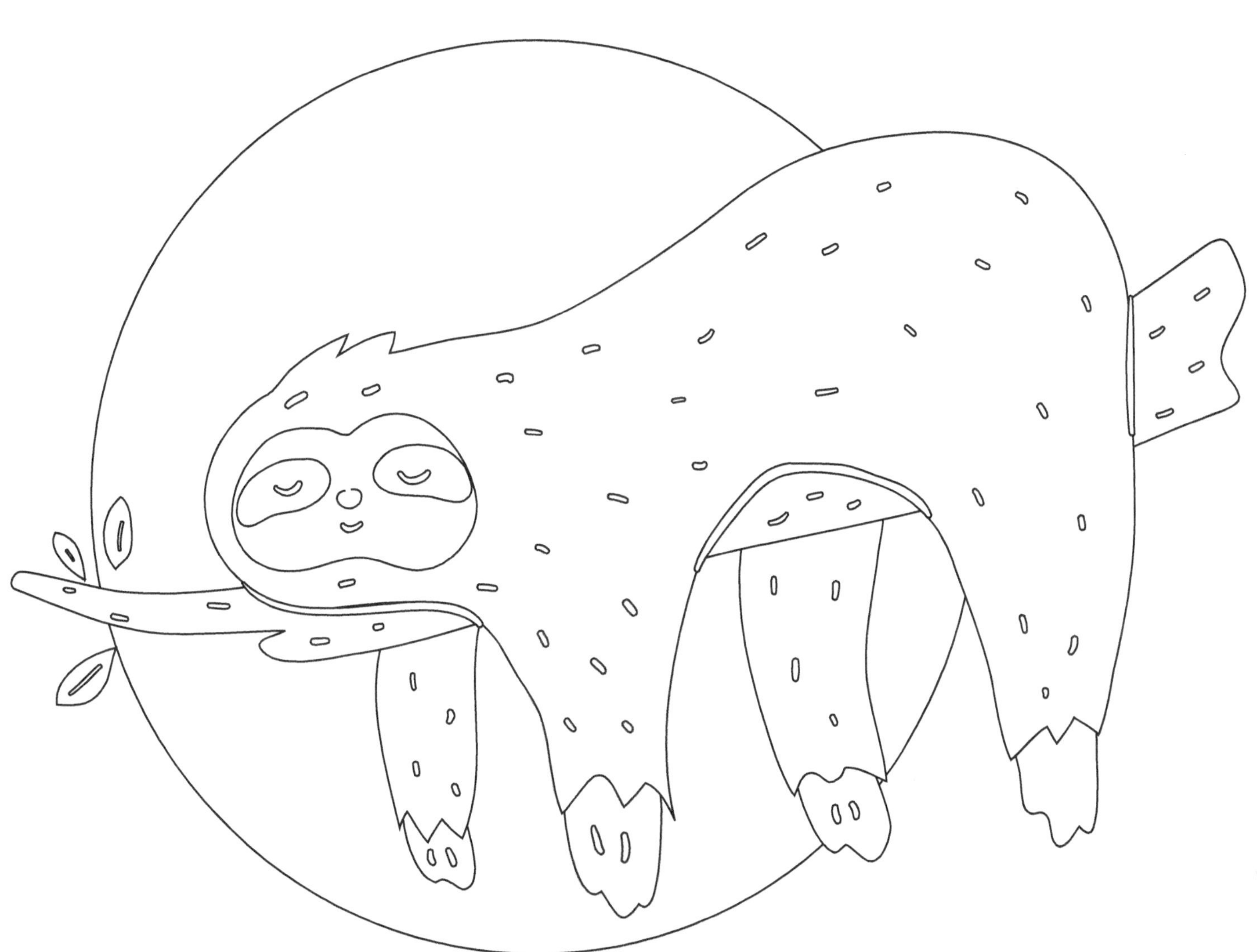

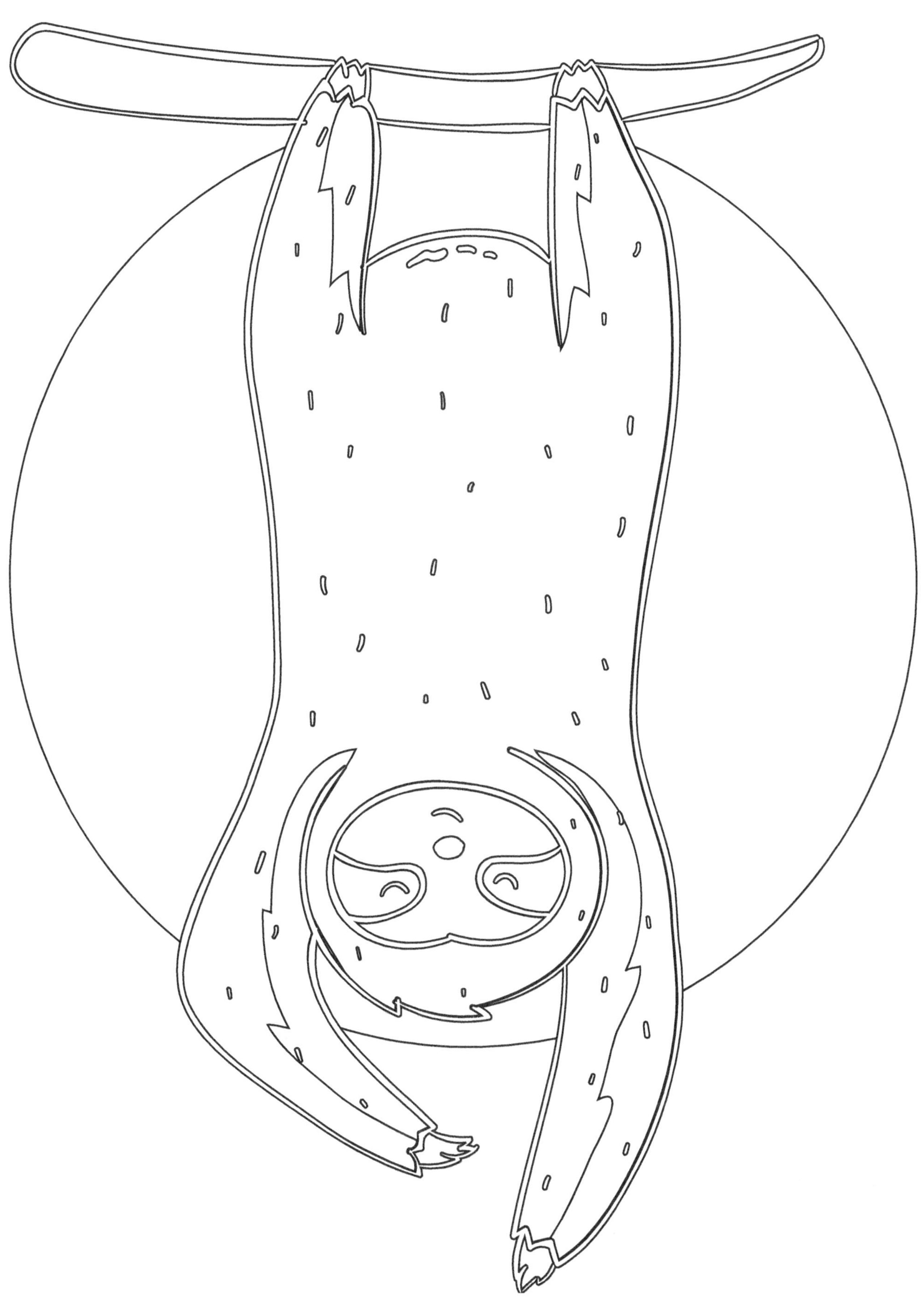

I HOPE

YOU LIKED THIS BOOK

9 7 9 8 6 6 6 4 6 7 0 9 1